2

Common Core State Standards

Second Grade Assessments

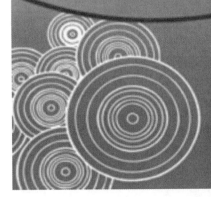

Grade 2

- **Math Standards**
- **English Standards**

Worksheets and Activities that assess every standard!

Table of Contents

Use your mouse to navigate through the workbook by clicking on the Standard.

2

Common Core State Standards

English Assessments

Grade 2

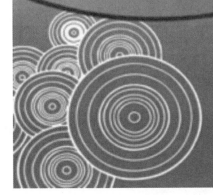

- **Math Standards**
- **English Standards**

Worksheets and Activities that assess every standard!

Name: _____ **Date:** _____

Directions: Read the story and answer the questions to show your understanding of the text.

Assessment

Eating Healthy

Ethan loved eating chicken nuggets, pizza, fries, and burgers. To drink, he always liked milk shakes, cola, or sugary drinks. The sweeter it was, the more he liked it. His mother said, "You eat too much sugar. Look at what you're eating for breakfast." Ethan looked at the food in front of him. He had juice, Rainbow Sugar Krispies, and a donut.

He took a bite of his glazed, jelly-filled donut. He chewed and then stopped when his teeth began to ache. "You're going to have to go to the dentist if you're getting cavities," Mom said. "Why do all the delicious things have to be bad for me? I can't eat broccoli forever. I'm not a rabbit," Ethan replied.

"I know, but you don't get all the vitamins and minerals you need from the stuff you like to eat. All that food is sugar and fat. You need good food for healthy teeth, eyes, and even your brain!" His mother explained. "If you can't start making healthy choices more often, I won't buy any junk food or sweets to keep in the house for snacks." Ethan frowned.

"Snacks are supposed to be occasional treats, not your regular meals. I should have bought more healthy breakfast foods for you. Tomorrow you will have eggs, toast without jam, bacon, some fresh fruit, and a glass of milk," His mom explained. "That doesn't sound too bad," Ethan replied.

"I'm not going to put all these sweets in your lunch anymore, either. You will get yogurt, raisins, or fresh fruit for your dessert in your lunch, okay?" Mom explained. Ethan didn't want to agree, but his mom's suggestion wasn't really that bad. Maybe his teeth wouldn't hurt so much anymore, either. He really didn't like trips to the dentist.

Answer these questions about the text.

1. When does this story take place?

_____

2. Who are the characters?

_____

3. Why does the mom want to change the foods that Ethan eats?

_____

4. What are some of the foods the mom wants Ethan to eat?

_____

_____

Ask a question about this text.

_____

_____

Name: _____ **Date:** _____

Directions: Read the fable below. Recount the story to show your understanding. What lesson or moral does this fable teach?

Assessment

The Lion and the Mouse

Once when a Lion was asleep, a little Mouse began running up and down upon him; this soon wakened the Lion, who placed his huge paw upon him, and opened his big jaws to swallow him. "Pardon, O King," cried the little Mouse: "Forgive me this time, I shall never forget it: Who knows, I may be able to do you a favor in return one of these days?"

The Lion was so tickled at the idea of the Mouse being able to help him, that he lifted up his paw and let him go. Some time after, the Lion was caught in a trap. The hunters who desired to carry him alive to the King tied him to a tree while they went in search of a wagon to carry him on. Just then, the little Mouse happened to pass by, and seeing the dangerous situation in which the Lion was, went up to him and soon gnawed away the ropes that bound the King of the Beasts. "Was I not right?" said the little Mouse.

How does the Lion feel about the Mouse at the beginning of this fable?
_____
_____

How does he feel by the end?
_____
_____

What lesson did the Lion learn?
_____
_____
_____
_____

What does this fable try to teach?
_____
_____
_____
_____

Name:_____   **Date:** _____

Directions: Read an assigned story. Think about the events that occur in the story, and how the character or characters react to these events. Write the words from the text that tell you about what the character says or does.

Assessment

Title: _____

Author: _____

Event	Character Reactions	Text Evidence

Name: _____ **Date:** _____

Directions: Read the poem below. Do you hear a rhythm? Do you hear the rhyme?

Assessment

Frozen ice cream in a cone,
fun with my friends, or alone.
Cold and icy, sweet and creamy,
on a hot day that is steamy.

Sun is shining, my ice cream drips,
melts down my arm and to my hips.
Lick it quickly, round and round.
Never let it hit the ground.

Answer these questions about the text.

1. Do you hear a rhythm in this poem? How many beats are in each line?

line 1 _____   line 5 _____
line 2 _____   line 6 _____
line 3 _____   line 7 _____
line 4 _____   line 8 _____

2. What rhyming words do you hear?

_____ _____   _____ _____

_____ _____   _____ _____

3. Can you write the next stanza?

_____

_____

_____

_____

Score _____

Name:_____ **Date:** _____

Directions: Read the assigned story. Think about the beginning and end of the story and the purpose of each. Write how the beginning of the story introduces the characters and main idea of the story. Write how the ending brings everything to a close, solves problems, and answers questions.

Assessment

The book I chose is:

_____

Written by:

_____

The beginning of the story introduces the characters and how they may interact.   It catches the reader's attention. What important things happen at the beginning to introduce the story to the reader?

_____

_____

_____

_____

_____

_____

The end of the story solves the problems that have occurred in the story and resolves events. What happens at the end of the story that brings the story to a close?

_____

_____

_____

_____

_____

_____

© http://CoreCommonStandards.com

Name:_____ **Date:**_____

Directions: Read, or listen to, the story *Hey, Little Ant*, by Phillip M. Hoose. Think about the different point of view each character has in the story.

Assessment

Describe the Boy's point of view...

Describe the Ant's point of view...

Now give YOUR point of view about the story...

Name: _____   **Date:** _____

Directions: Select a storybook to read. Use the illustrations and the text to understand the characters, setting, and plot. Choose an illustration to reproduce below. The illustration should represent a character, setting, or an event in the story. Describe how the illustration, and story text, helps you to better understand an element from the story.

Assessment

My illustration shows a: (setting) (character) (event).

circle one

Here's how the illustration and text from the book help me understand the story:

_____
_____
_____
_____
_____
_____
_____
_____
_____
_____
_____
_____
_____

Name:_____   **Date:** _____

Directions: Read two stories with similar plots, or characters. Compare the elements from the two stories below.

Assessment - Page 1

Title #1: _____

Title #2: _____

Compare Characters

Compare Settings

© http://CoreCommonStandards.com

Score [   ]

Name:_____ **Date:** _____

Directions: Read two stories with similar plots, or characters. Compare the elements from the two stories below.

Assessment - Page 2

Title #1:

Title #2:

_____

_____

Compare Problems

Compare Solutions

© http://CoreCommonStandards.com

Name: _____ **Date:** _____

Directions: Read various types of prose and poetry at your level. Record the titles. Try to read at least one book of every genre. Lightly color in each star after you have read a book of that type.

Assessment

Fairy Tale

Book Title:
_____

Poetry

Book Title:
_____

Picture Book

Book Title:
_____

Fantasy

Book Title:
_____

Realistic Fiction

Book Title:
_____

Your Choice

Book Title:
_____

Name:_____ **Date:** _____

Directions: Read the story and answer the questions to show your understanding of the text.

Assessment

Giraffes

The giraffe is one of the world's tallest mammals. They are known for their long necks, long legs, and spotted body. Giraffes have small horns at the top of their heads that grow to be about 5 inches. These knobs are used to protect from an enemy.

Male giraffes are taller than female giraffes and can stand nearly 19 feet tall. Most giraffes can live up to 25 years in the wild. They like to roam around in the savannas of Africa. African savannas are mainly dry and are covered with grass.

With the giraffe's neck being so long, they are able to eat leaves from tall acacia trees. Giraffes can go many days without drinking water and can live by eating wet leaves.

Answer these questions about the text.

1. Where do most giraffes live?

_____

2. Which giraffe grows taller; the male or the female? How tall?

_____

3. How do giraffes get water if there are no water sources around?

_____

4. What do giraffes look like?

_____

_____

Ask two questions about this text.

_____

_____

_____

Name: _____ **Date:** _____

Directions: Read the passage below. What is the main topic of the text? What is the focus of each paragraph?

Assessment

Piñatas

The piñata is a tradition of Mexico. A piñata is a clay pot filled with candy, fruit, and confetti. It is decorated with tinsel, ribbons, and colored paper. Mexican children love piñatas and enjoy them at Christmas, birthdays, and fiestas.

A rope is thrown over a branch and then tied to the piñata. Usually, an adult pulls the rope causing the piñata to go up and down while a child tries to hit it with a stick and break it open. Children take turns hitting the piñata to get to its prize.

American children sometimes enjoy piñatas that are made of paper mâché and decorated with crêpe paper. Once it is busted open, kids race to grab the candy that falls to the ground.

Main Topic of This Text:

Main Focus of Paragraph 1:

Main Focus of Paragraph 2:

Main Focus of Paragraph 3:

Name: _____   **Date:** _____

Directions: After reading an informational story and discussing the events of the story, choose two events that occur. Write one way that each event is unique from the other. Then write a piece of information that is common to both.

Assessment

Story: _____

Author: _____

Event 1 _____   **Event 2** _____

_____   _____

_____   _____

_____   _____

Something unique about this event.   **Something unique about this event.**

_____   _____

_____   _____

_____   _____

_____   _____

Something both events have in common.

_____

_____

_____

_____

Name: _____ **Date:** _____

Directions: Read *The Magic School Bus Lost in the Solar System.* Read the words from the text below. Use picture clues and context to determine the meanings of the words and phrases.

Assessment A

Word or Phrase

What I Think It Means...

orbit

The information I used from the text to help me

Word or Phrase

What I Think It Means...

atmosphere

The information I used from the text to help me

Word or Phrase

What I Think It Means...

asteroid belt

The information I used from the text to help me

Score

Name:_____ **Date:** _____

Directions: Read an informational story. Choose vocabulary from the story to write in the chart below. Use picture clues and context to determine the meanings of the words and phrases.

Assessment B

Word or Phrase

What I Think It Means...

The information I used from the text to help me

Word or Phrase

What I Think It Means...

The information I used from the text to help me

Word or Phrase

What I Think It Means...

The information I used from the text to help me

Score _____

Name:_____ **Date:** _____

Directions: Choose an informational book or magazine to read. As you read, find examples of nonfiction text features. Look for things such as bold face type, italics, captions, headings, drawings, charts, and diagrams. Write or draw examples of the features you find, include page numbers, or cut and paste actual examples.

Assessment

Title of Book or Magazine:
_____

Heading	**Caption**	**Index**
Page #	Page #	Page #
Diagram	**Photo**	**Chart**
Page #	Page #	Page #
Bold Type	**Italics**	**Glossary**
Page #	Page #	Page #

Name: _____   **Date:** _____

Directions: Choose an informational text to read. Think about the author's purpose for writing the passage. Identify the main purpose and tell what the author wants to answer, explain, or describe.

Assessment

Text Title:

_____

Author:

_____

Topic:

_____

Type of Text:

_____

What is the purpose for this text? What is the author trying to explain, describe, or answer?

_____

_____

_____

Cite some details from the text the author uses to support his/her ideas.

_____

_____

_____

_____

Do you agree with the author? Why or why not?

_____

_____

Score

Name:_____ **Date:** _____

Directions: Images in books and magazines help us to better understand the information the author is trying to convey. Look at the images below. How do you think they would contribute to and clarify a text? What could you learn from these images?

Assessment

image photograph n diagram n drawing	How does the image add to the text or help the reader better understand the text?	What could you learn from the image?
 What kind of image is this? _____		
 What kind of image is this? _____		
 What kind of image is this? _____		

Name:_____ **Date:**_____

Directions: Read the passage below about bowling. What are the reasons the author gives for bowling being a fun and worthwhile sport?

Assessment

Bowling is a Great Way to Spend a Saturday

Bowling is a fun sport. I love the sound of the ball when it hits the shiny, wooden lane. The ball spins as it rolls for the 10 white pins. Then "crack," like a thunder clap, the ball collides with the pins and sends them sailing. You get to wear these really colorful shoes that slip and slide as you hurl the ball on each of your rolls.

Scoring in bowling is very interesting. For each pin you knock down, you get a point. If you knock all ten down in two rolls, you get a spare, and make a slash on the score card. If you knock all ten down in one shot, you get a strike, which is a big, fat X! We used to keep track of the pins we knock down by writing our scores on a large piece of paper with lots of lines. Now, many bowling lanes have computers do all the scoring for you. I liked writing the scores myself, because I got to practice my addition skills!

If you aren't a great runner, or too accurate with hitting a ball, then bowling may be a good sport for you. My friend plays and has three trophies! It takes good aim and skill to line the ball up to hit those pins, especially with the dreaded 7 - 10 split. That's when the back left and back right pins are all that are left standing, with a big gaping hole in between. If you can hit those, bowling might be the sport for you!

Fun with friends and family, using math skills, and it's just a cool sport. Bowling is a great way to spend a Saturday!

What reasons does the author give to say that you would may enjoy bowling?

Name:_____ **Date:**_____

Directions: After reading two different texts about the same topic, complete the chart to compare and contrast the most important point of the text.

Assessment

What is the important point both texts are trying to make?

_____

_____

Texts I Read	Ways the texts are similar in how the point was presented.	Ways the texts are different in how the point was presented.
Text One _____ _____ **Topic** _____		
Text One _____ _____ **Topic** _____		

Do you think the texts proved their points?

_____

Score _____

Name: _____ **Date:** _____

Directions: Read various types of informational text at your level. Record the titles. Try to read at least one book of every genre. Lightly color in each star after you have read a book of that type.

Assessment

Animals & Plants

Book Title: _____
_____

People & Places

Book Title: _____
_____

Weather & Nature

Book Title: _____
_____

Earth & Space

Book Title: _____
_____

Biography & History

Book Title: _____
_____

Your Choice

Book Title: _____
_____

Name: _____   **Date:** _____

Directions: Read the words below. Determine if they have a long vowel or short vowel sound. Circle **long** or **short** for each word.

Assessment A

street	long short	spin	long short
kite	long short	flute	long short
flame	long short	scope	long short
stun	long short	brand	long short
stop	long short	tent	long short

Directions: Match the vowel team to the correct picture with that vowel sound and spelling.

ow   ee

aw   ay

ea   oa

oo   ey

ie   ue

Score [   ]

Name: _____ **Date:** _____

Directions: Read the two-syllable, long vowel words below aloud to your teacher, or a partner. Color the star if you read the word correctly.

Assessment B

Word	Star	Word	Star
actor	☆	wagon	☆
lobster	☆	follow	☆
planet	☆	table	☆
honey	☆	garden	☆
pumpkin	☆	thunder	☆

Directions: Read the words below that have prefixes and suffixes. Read them aloud to your teacher or a partner. Color the star if you read the word correctly.

Word	Star	Word	Star
dislike	☆	painless	☆
misprint	☆	smoothly	☆
prepare	☆	colorful	☆
untie	☆	weakness	☆
renew	☆	smallest	☆

How did you do? When you read a story, text, or other type of writing, look for multi-syllable words, and words with prefixes and suffixes.

Second Grade Common Core Assessment

© http://CoreCommonStandards.com

Name: _____   **Date:** _____

Directions: Read the words below aloud to your teacher. Notice that the words have the same vowel spellings, but these spellings have different sounds. Color the star if you have read the word correctly.

Assessment C

your	☆	field	☆
rough	☆	friend	☆
group	☆	fierce	☆
ouch	☆	window	☆
pie	☆	clown	☆

Directions: Read the words below aloud to your teacher. These words are common words that don't follow normal spelling rules.

said	☆	many	☆
what	☆	often	☆
whose	☆	their	☆
should	☆	word	☆
people	☆	enough	☆

How did you do? When you read a story, text, or other type of writing, look for inconsistent vowel spellings and irregularly spelled words.

Name:_____   **Date:** _____

Directions: Read with sufficient accuracy and fluency to support comprehension.

Assessment

Title:_____

Level:_____ Shows comprehension:_____

Error Rate: Total Words:_____ / Errors:_____ ER = 1:_____

Self Correction Rate: Total Errors + Total SC / Total SC: _____ = 1:_____

Accuracy Rate: (Total Words - Total Errors)/Total words x 100 = _____ %

Rate of Fluency: Total WPM _____ Total Errors: _____ WCPM: _____

Retelling: _____

_____

Areas of concern: _____

_____

Student Skills Checklist

 Student comprehends reading.

 Student read most words correctly.

 Student read with expression.

 Student self-corrected most errors.

 Student used context to guess a word(s).

Name: _____ **Date:** _____

Directions: Read with sufficient accuracy and fluency to support comprehension.

Assessment

Running Record

As the student reads aloud a benchmark text, keep track of the errors and self-corrections the student makes.

- √ correct words
- record errors by writing the *replacement* or *skipped* word above the actual word
- write *R* when the child repeats a word or phrase
- write *SC* above any word or phrase that is self-corrected
- tick off the errors and self corrections (SC) to the right of the text using tallies ///
- add the errors and self-corrections
- use these totals to calculate the error rate, accuracy rate, and self-correction rate

Calculate the error rate
The error rate is expressed as a ratio and is calculated by using this formula:
Total words / Total errors = Error rate
(ex: 100/4 = 25   ER = 1:25) {student read 25 words correctly for every one error made}

Calculate the accuracy rate
The accuracy rate is expressed as a percentage. You calculate the accuracy rate using this formula:
[Total words read - Total errors] / Total words read x 100 = Accuracy rate
(ex: [100-4]/100 x 100 = 96 AR = 96%)

Accuracy Rate Chart
Independent: 95% - 100%
Instructional: 90% - 94%
Frustrational: 89% and below

Calculate the self-correction rate
The self-correction rate is expressed as a ratio and can be calculated by using this formula:
(Number of errors + Number of self corrections) / Number of self corrections = SC rate
(ex: [4 + 6]/6 = 1.67 or 2 (round to nearest whole number) SC = 1:2) {student self-corrects 1 out of every 2 words}

Fluency

Using a passage that is a fluency benchmark, or is appropriately leveled, the student will read for one minute. Tally the number of errors, not the type of error. Encourage the student to read as many words as possible and not treat this as a running record by going back and rereading.

Calculate the number of WPM (Words Per Minute) - Errors = WCPM (Words Correct Per Minute)
Use this standard rate chart to score.

Grade 1 ... 80 wcpm	Grade 4 ... 140 wcpm
Grade 2 ... 90 wcpm	Grade 5 ... 150 wcpm
Grade 3 ... 110 wcpm	Grade 6 ... 180 wcpm

Name:_____   **Date:**_____

Directions: Read a book or article and write an opinion about the topic. Cite evidence from the text to support your opinion. Use words such as *because* and *also* to connect opinions and reasons.

Assessment

The text I read is titled_____.

This text is about _____.

My opinion about this text is: _____

_____

_____

Here are the reasons that support my opinion: _____

_____

_____

_____

_____

In conclusion, my opinion is _____

_____

_____

Name:_____ **Date:** _____

Directions: Plan writing for an informative or explanatory text on this page. Introduce a topic and use facts and details to make your writing true. Be sure to include a concluding statement. Write a complete draft on page 2.

Assessment - Page 1

My topic: _____

FACT:	DETAIL:
_____ _____	_____ _____

FACT:	DETAIL:
_____ _____	_____ _____

FACT:	DETAIL:
_____ _____	_____ _____

Conclusion:

_____

_____

Score

Name:_____ **Date:** _____

Directions: Using your planning from page 1, write an informative or explanatory text. Introduce a topic and use facts and details to make your writing true. Be sure to include a concluding statement.

Assessment - Page 2

Name: _____ **Date:** _____

Directions: On this page, plan to write a narrative that tells about an event that you experienced or read about. Include details to describe actions, thoughts, and feelings. Write a draft on page 2.

Assessment - Page 1

My story: _____

EVENT:	DETAIL:
_____ _____	_____ _____

EVENT:	DETAIL:
_____ _____	_____ _____

EVENT:	DETAIL:
_____ _____	_____ _____

Conclusion:
_____
_____

Name:_____ **Date:**_____

Directions: Using the planner from page 1, write a narrative that tells about an event that you experienced or read about. Include details to describe actions, thoughts, and feelings. Write about the events in order, and provide a sense of closure.

Assessment - Page 2

Name:_____ **Date:** _____

Directions: After completing a piece of writing, work with peers and adults to strengthen your writing by editing and revising.

Assessment

My topic: _____

I edited my writing for...

proper use of capital letters

punctuation   .   !   ?   ,   ""

spelling of common words

full sentences

a beginning, middle, and end

I revised my writing to...

use vivid verbs to explain action

use descriptive adjectives

explain thoughts and feelings

provide facts and evidence

focus on the topic

Name:_____ **Date:** _____

Directions: Record the digital tools your students use. Print multiple pages for use with entire class.

Assessment

Digital Skill	Date	Notes
Can turn on a computer.		
Can shut down a computer.		
Uses a mouse well. (Can double-click; move cursor to desired place; scroll if available.)		
Knows where most common characters are on keyboard.		
Can log in and out of programs.		
Can change the font or size of font.		
Knows how to use space bar; back space; delete; and return.		
Can add a graphic.		
Can drag and drop an item.		
Can copy/paste an item.		
Can save a file.		
Can print work.		
Can print a file.		
Can use word processing and/or presentation software to type and create resources.		

Name:_____ **Date:** _____

Directions: Participate in a shared research project. Choose a topic and use various books to study the topic. Or, record science observations to learn more about your topic.

Assessment

My partner(s): _____

Our research topic: _____

What we want to learn or teach: _____

_____

The resources we used:

_____   _____

_____   _____

Things that we observed:

_____

_____

Something that surprised us: _____

_____

_____

How we will present our project: _____

_____

_____

Name:_____   **Date:** _____

Directions: Compose a question about a topic you are are studying in school. Use resources to gather information to answer the question. Then, write your answer citing the evidence that you found.

Assessment

The question I have is:

_____

_____

To answer my question, I will use these resources:

⭐ informational book   ⭐ observation

⭐ reference book   ⭐ internet search

⭐ magazine or journal   ⭐ interview

My answer and the evidence I found:

_____
_____
_____
_____
_____
_____
_____
_____
_____
_____
_____

Name: _____   **Date:** _____

Directions: Participate in a group discussion. Follow agreed-upon rules of collaboration. Use this organizer to take notes of others' ideas, your own thoughts, and what you learned.

Assessment

☆ I wait my turn to speak   ☆ I ask meaningful questions

☆ I respect others' ideas   ☆ I stay on topic

☆ I listen when others talk   ☆ I offer ideas and suggestions

What others are saying...

_____

_____

_____

_____

_____

_____

My thoughts about the topic...

_____

_____

_____

_____

_____

_____

What I learned from this discussion...

_____

_____

_____

_____

_____

Name: _____ **Date:** _____

Directions: Read text or listen to an oral presentation and take notes on the details or key ideas you hear. Tell the main idea of the information.

Assessment

Text or presentation topic: _____

Source: Title of Text or Name of Presenter: _____

Here is a detail or key idea I noticed...

_____

_____

Here is a detail or key idea I noticed...

_____

_____

Here is a detail or key idea I noticed...

_____

_____

Here is a detail or key idea I noticed...

_____

_____

What is the main idea of the information read or presented?

_____

_____

Name:_____ **Date:** _____

Directions: Listen to a speaker present a topic. Ask questions that will help you better understand the information, or gather additional information.

Assessment

Text or presentation topic: _____

Presenter: _____

Here is a question that I asked:

_____

_____

_____

I asked this question to...

☐ better understand the information ☐ get more information

Here is the answer I was given:

_____

_____

_____

What is the main idea of the information presented?

_____

_____

Name:_____ **Date:** _____

Directions: Tell a story you've made up or heard, or share an experience you have had. Use facts, details, and speak clearly. Plan your story using this organizer.

Assessment

My story or experience is about: _____

_____

_____

_____

Something that happened:

_____

_____

Descriptive details:

_____

_____

_____

Something that happened

_____

_____

Descriptive details:

_____

_____

_____

Something that happened:

_____

_____

Descriptive details:

_____

_____

_____

Something that happened:

_____

_____

Descriptive details:

_____

_____

_____

Name:_____ **Date:** _____

Directions: Record yourself telling a story or reciting a poem. Add visual displays to help your recording come alive.
Play your recording for your peers.

Assessment

The story or poem I will record is: _____

_____

It was written by: _____

I used a _____ to make my recording.

When I recorded, I...

☆ spoke clearly   ☆ used descriptive words

☆ used different voices   ☆ used descriptive verbs

☆ changed my volume   ☆ enjoyed storytelling

I added visuals to my storytelling.

Here is what I added:

☆ drawings   ☆ historical objects

☆ clipart   ☆ book illustrations

☆ photographs   ☆ diagrams/charts

☆ 3D models   ☆ _____

Name:_____ **Date:** _____

Directions: When you speak, produce complete sentences so people can fully understand what you want to say. When you hear yourself using compete sentences in different situations, fill in a star as a reward.

Assessment

I speak in complete sentences when...

providing details

giving directions

retelling a story

sharing information

asking questions

getting clarification

explaining something

asking permission

© http://CoreCommonStandards.com

Name:_____ **Date:** _____

Directions: Choose the proper collective noun for each sentence.

Assessment A

1. The speaker presented to the _____ of students.

   class   band   team

2. The _____ of birds startled me when they flew off.

   litter   flock   hive

3. The boss asked his _____ to meet with him before work.

   gang   tribe   staff

4. I selected from the neat _____ of books on the table.

   stack   bunch   fleet

5. Dad surprised mom with a beautiful _____ of roses!

   galaxy   album   bouquet

Directions: Choose the proper reflexive noun for each sentence.

1. I was very proud of _____ after I gave my speech.

   myself   yourself   itself

2. You should pace _____ or you will be finished too quickly.

   ourselves   themselves   yourselves

3. She allowed _____ one chocolate brownie as a reward.

   himself   herself   themselves

4. I laughed as I watched the hamster clean _____.

   itself   themselves   ourselves

5. Steve asked _____ if he was ready to ski the slopes.

   myself   herself   himself

Name:_____ **Date:** _____

Directions: Choose the proper irregular noun for each sentence.

Assessment B

1. There were five _____ working on the old car.

         man   **men**   **mans**   **mens**

2. I can see one _____ dancing on the stage.

     person   **peoples**   **persons**   **people**

3. At night we can hear all of the _____ running around.

     mouse   **mice**   **mouses**   **mices**

4. The bus was full of _____ heading to the zoo.

     childrens   **childs**   **children**   **child**

5. A cute, little _____ follows me around the pond.

     gooses   **geeses**   **geese**   **goose**

6. My dad likes to soak both his _____ at night.

     foot   **feet**   **feets**   **foots**

7. I may have to go to the dentist to pull out a _____.

     tooth   **teeths**   **teeth**   **tooths**

8. Twenty-four _____ were at my uncle's farm.

     oxes   **oxen**   **oxens**   **ox**

9. I asked the _____ if she could help me find a dress.

     womans   **women**   **woman**   **womens**

10. We counted 10 _____ in our aquarium.

     fish   **fishs**   **fishes**   **feesh**

Score _____

Name: _____ **Date:** _____

Directions: Choose the proper irregular verb for each sentence.

Assessment C

1. Susie _____ her book report late last night.

                    begin   **began**   **begined**

2. You knocked over mom's new vase and it _____!

                    break   **breaked**   **broke**

3. The kids had _____ a huge Lego castle in the kitchen.

                    built   **builded**   **build**

4. Bob's little sister, Mary, _____ all over the wall with crayon!

                    drawed   **draw**   **drew**

5. The students _____ each others' hands as they walked.

                    held   **hold**   **holded**

Directions: Choose the proper adjective or adverb for each sentence.

1. The little boy _____ walked home from the baseball game.

                    sad   **sadly**

2. My hamster moved _____ through the maze I built.

                    quickly   **quick**

3. The _____ young man held the door open for the woman.

                    kind   **kindly**

4. Patty moved _____ through the briar bushes.

                    careful   **carefully**

5. We were the _____ students to get a slice of pizza.

                    final   **finally**

Score [_____]

Name:_____ **Date:** _____

Directions: Read the sentences below. Rewrite each sentence, or set of sentences, to make them more complex. Combine and expand sentences by adding adjectives, adverbs, and more interesting nouns and verbs.

Assessment D

1. Sally runs fast. She is in a race.

   _____
   _____
   _____
   _____
   _____

2. The cat makes noise at night.

   _____
   _____
   _____
   _____
   _____

3. We watched a movie. It was scary.

   _____
   _____
   _____
   _____
   _____

4. I opened my gift. I was happy.

   _____
   _____
   _____
   _____
   _____

5. Mom drinks her coffee in a mug.

   _____
   _____
   _____
   _____
   _____

Name: _____   **Date:** _____

Directions: Read the letter below. Correct the missing capitals, commas, and apostrophes.

Assessment A

Dear Carlos

   I am writing to tell you that last week I bought a

new bicycle. It isnt really new. It used to be Bennys

bike, but he bought a new schwinn at joes bike shop in

east harlem. Benny knew I had asked for a bike for

christmas, but I didnt get one. Wasnt he nice to do

that?   Now I can give my old bike to Sean before he

moves to new jersey. Seans bike was stolen last

month along with his dell computer. Hes upset, and I

know this will make him happy! Talk to you soon!

                   Your Friend

                   Pedro

Name: _____ **Date:** _____

Directions: Write words that fit the common spelling patterns below.

Assessment B

ick	udge	art

eat	oat	ight

Name:_____ **Date:** _____

Directions: Use reference materials when you need them. Color a star every time you use the reference materials listed below.

Assessment C

Dictionary

Thesaurus

Search Engine

Atlas

Encyclopedia

Name:_____ **Date:** _____

Directions: Sometimes we use formal language when we speak and write; sometimes we use informal language. Read the situations below. Circle formal or informal to show what kind of language might be used. For the sentences that are written in informal language, rewrite them in a formal way.

Assessment

1. No way! That's so cool! You got an A!

formal
informal

2. Hello. It is my pleasure to meet you.

formal
informal

3. Would you like a cup of tea, ma'am?

formal
informal

4. Hey, see ya later, dude.

formal
informal

5. Please speak quietly in the library.

formal
informal

Name:_____ **Date:** _____

Directions: Read the root words below. What does each word mean? How does adding a few letters to the root word change the meaning?

Assessment A

Read the root words below. What does each word mean?
What does each word mean after a prefix has been added?

root	meaning	new word	new meaning
happy		unhappy	
heat		preheat	
write		rewrite	
like		dislike	
polite		impolite	

Read the root words below. What does each word mean?
Use the root word's meaning to help you understand the new word.

root	meaning	new word	new meaning
addition		additional	
comfort		comfortable	
mountain		mountaineer	
cheer		cheerily	
impress		impression	

Score _____

Name:_____ **Date:** _____

Directions: Read the words below. Think about the meaning of each word. Then, combine the words and determine the meaning of the new compound word.

Assessment B

Read the words below. Think about what each word means.
When you combine the two words, what does the new compound word mean?

word	word	compound word	new meaning
fire	fly		
pea	nut		
hand	some		
book	shelf		
bird	house		

Use the clues in the sentence to understand the meaning of the underlined word.

1. I **hastily** did my homework to finish it on time.

I think **hastily** means:
_____

2. Ben was so hungry, he **consumed** the entire pizza!

I think **consumed** means:
_____

3. Sparky was **obedient** and did what he was told.

I think **obedient** means:
_____

4. Since it started to rain, we **altered** our picnic plans.

I think **altered** means:
_____

5. He crumpled the paper and **discarded** it into the trash.

I think **discarded** means:
_____

Name: _____ **Date:** _____

Directions: Read the lists of verbs and adjectives below. Write them in order of intensity from least to greatest.

Assessment

stare   look   glance   peek

_____ _____ _____ _____

say   scream   whisper   shout

_____ _____ _____ _____

big   tiny   huge   small

_____ _____ _____ _____

smack   poke   tap   punch

_____ _____ _____ _____

bright   dim   brilliant   shiny

_____ _____ _____ _____

Directions: Write things that you think of when you read the descriptive words below.

<u>Things that are soft.</u>	<u>Things that are tiny.</u>	<u>Things that are fast.</u>

Score _____

Name: _____ **Date:** _____

Directions: When we read, listen, and speak, we collect words. Keep track of the great words you learn that can help you describe your feelings and actions.

Assessment

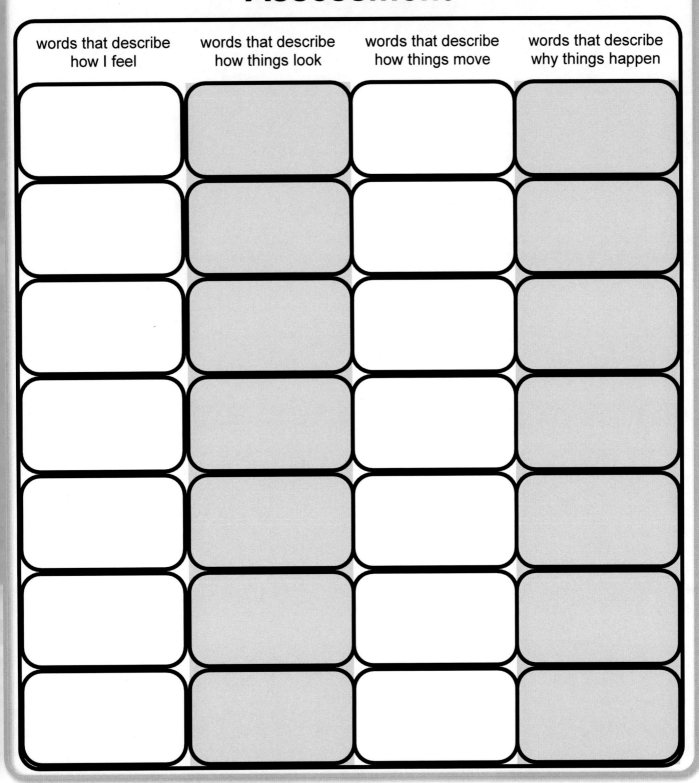

words that describe how I feel	words that describe how things look	words that describe how things move	words that describe why things happen

2

Common Core State Standards

Math Assessments

Grade 2

- **Math Standards**
- **English Standards**

Worksheets and Activities that assess every standard!

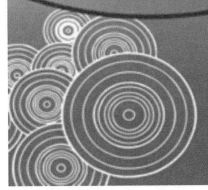

Name:_____ **Date:** _____

Directions: Read the number stories below. Think about what information is important. Think about whether you should add or subtract. Draw pictures and equations to help you work out the problems.

Assessment

My blue jewelry box has 15 rings. Julie's red jewelry box has 11 rings. How many rings do we have altogether?

_____rings

Bob and Brady each have markers in their school bag. Bob has 26 markers. Brady has 31 markers. How many more markers does Brady have?

_____markers

Last night, I left 56 pieces of bread out on the picnic table. This morning, there were only 24 pieces left. How many pieces of bread were eaten by the birds?

_____bread

Friday I baked 2 dozen cookies. Saturday I baked 3 dozen cookies. My dad ate half a dozen. How many cookies were left?

_____cookies

At 9:00am, the temperature was 67°F. By noon, it was 89°F. How many degrees did the temperature rise?

_____degrees

Score

Name:_____ **Date:** _____

Directions: Know how to add and subtract within 20. Solve the addition and subtraction equations below.
Use strategies you know to find answers.

Assessment

$$
\begin{array}{r} 8 \\ +\ 4 \\ \hline \end{array}
\qquad
\begin{array}{r} 7 \\ +\ 7 \\ \hline \end{array}
\qquad
\begin{array}{r} 9 \\ +\ 5 \\ \hline \end{array}
\qquad
\begin{array}{r} 8 \\ +\ 6 \\ \hline \end{array}
$$

$$
\begin{array}{r} 19 \\ -\ 9 \\ \hline \end{array}
\qquad
\begin{array}{r} 17 \\ -\ 3 \\ \hline \end{array}
\qquad
\begin{array}{r} 15 \\ -\ 8 \\ \hline \end{array}
\qquad
\begin{array}{r} 20 \\ -\ 11 \\ \hline \end{array}
$$

8 + 7 = ☐   4 + 9 = ☐   7 + 5 = ☐

15 - 7 = ☐   13 - 9 = ☐   19 - 8 = ☐

Name:_____   **Date:** _____

Directions: Read the numbers below. Color the odd numbers blue. Color the even numbers red.

Assessment A

13	10	60	54	11
27	15	18	78	29
41	24	73	8	1
83	92	72	9	77

Directions: Choose 4 even numbers and use each one as an answer to the problems below. Write an equation to express each even number as a sum of two equal addends.

+ =	+ =
+ =	+ =

Name: _____ **Date:** _____

Directions: Count the number of objects in each set. Write that number on the line. Then decide if this is an odd or even number. If it is odd, add one more to the set to make it even. Finally, write an equation that expresses the even number as the sum of two equal addends.

Assessment B

SAMPLE

  7   (odd)   4 + 4 = 8
___   even   ___   ___

   odd

___   even   ___ + ___ = ___

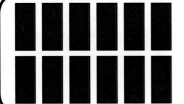   odd

___   even   ___ + ___ = ___

   odd

___   even   ___ + ___ = ___

   odd

___   even   ___ + ___ = ___

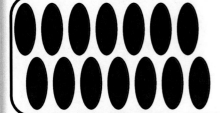   odd

___   even   ___ + ___ = ___

Name:_____ **Date:** _____

Directions: Look at the arrays below. For each array, use two colors to fill int he squares. Then write an addition equation using the number of squares of each color as the addends and the total number of squares in the array as the sum.

Assessment

Name:_____   **Date:** _____

Directions: Read the numbers below. Write the amount of ones, tens, and hundreds that are in each number.

Assessment

457
____hundreds
____ones
____tens

102
____ones
____tens
____hundreds

735
____tens
____ones
____hundreds

229
____ones
____tens
____hundreds

310
____ones
____hundreds
____tens

864
____ones
____tens
____hundreds

983
____tens
____ones
____hundreds

658
____ones
____tens
____hundreds

517
____hundreds
____ones
____tens

Name:_____ **Date:** _____

Directions: Count aloud within 1000. Count by 1's from the start number to the finish number.

Assessment

Count aloud from: **245** to: **307**

Count aloud from: **420** to: **463**

Count aloud from: **951** to: **1000**

Directions: Continue the skip counts. Some count by 5's, 10's, or 100's.

70	75			95						

	55							90		

			20	30						

						60	70			

			400		600					

Name:_____   **Date:** _____

Directions: Listen to your teacher say a number. Write each number using base-ten numerals, number names in written form, and expanded form.

Assessment

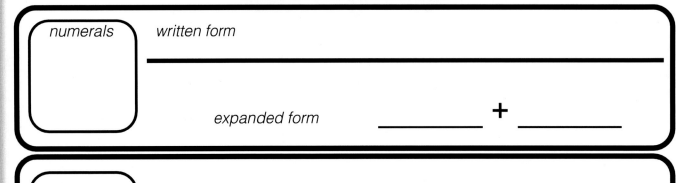

numerals

written form

_____

expanded form   _____ + _____

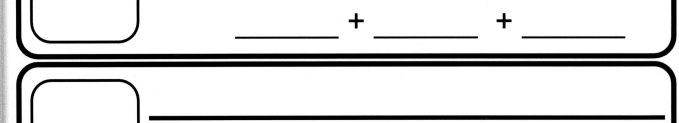

_____ + _____ + _____

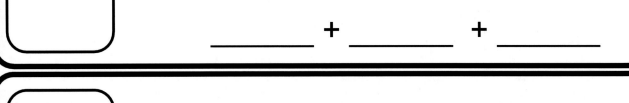

_____ + _____ + _____

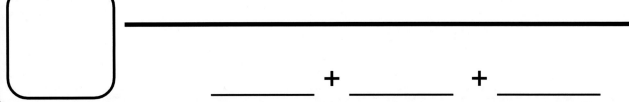

_____ + _____ + _____

_____ + _____ + _____

Name:_____   **Date:** _____

Directions: Compare the three-digit numbers below. Write the symbols < , > , or = to record the results of the comparisons.

Assessment

1.

459 ___ 195

6.

129 ___ 129

2.

308 ___ 396

7.

636 ___ 363

3.

440 ___ 439

8.

220 ___ 660

4.

388 ___ 388

9.

474 ___ 747

5.

503 ___ 703

10.

989 ___ 999

© http://CoreCommonStandards.com

Name:_____ **Date:** _____

Directions: Know how to add to and subtract within 100. Solve the addition and subtraction equations below. Use strategies you know.

Assessment

$$\begin{array}{r} 45 \\ + 11 \\ \hline \end{array}$$

$$\begin{array}{r} 83 \\ + 7 \\ \hline \end{array}$$

$$\begin{array}{r} 29 \\ +30 \\ \hline \end{array}$$

$$\begin{array}{r} 66 \\ +23 \\ \hline \end{array}$$

$$\begin{array}{r} 89 \\ - 23 \\ \hline \end{array}$$

$$\begin{array}{r} 95 \\ - 34 \\ \hline \end{array}$$

$$\begin{array}{r} 67 \\ - 42 \\ \hline \end{array}$$

$$\begin{array}{r} 44 \\ -31 \\ \hline \end{array}$$

12 + 33 = ☐

54 + 10 = ☐

61 + 27 = ☐

54 - 21 = ☐

82 - 41 = ☐

89 - 8 = ☐

Name: _____ **Date:** _____

Directions: Add the two-digit numbers below. Use strategies you know such as place value and properties of operations to find the answers.

Assessment

1.
$$\begin{array}{r} 25 \\ 11 \\ +\ 10 \\ \hline \end{array}$$

2.
$$\begin{array}{r} 45 \\ 22 \\ +\ 10 \\ \hline \end{array}$$

3.
$$\begin{array}{r} 55 \\ 10 \\ +\ 13 \\ \hline \end{array}$$

4.
$$\begin{array}{r} 55 \\ 18 \\ +\ 13 \\ \hline \end{array}$$

5.
$$\begin{array}{r} 50 \\ 23 \\ 41 \\ +\ 32 \\ \hline \end{array}$$

6.
$$\begin{array}{r} 22 \\ 41 \\ 30 \\ +\ 15 \\ \hline \end{array}$$

7.
$$\begin{array}{r} 33 \\ 11 \\ 20 \\ +\ 12 \\ \hline \end{array}$$

8.
$$\begin{array}{r} 31 \\ 44 \\ 25 \\ +\ 13 \\ \hline \end{array}$$

Score

Name:_____ **Date:** _____

Directions: Add the three-digit numbers together by adding the ones, tens, and hundreds.

Assessment - A

1.

Th	H	T	O
	5	3	7
+	2	4	2

_____

,

2.

Th	H	T	O
	6	5	8
+	2	0	1

_____

,

3.

Th	H	T	O
	3	2	6
+	1	1	8

_____

,

4.

Th	H	T	O
	7	5	6
+	4	8	6

_____

,

5. $539 + 256 + 103 =$ _____

Score _____

Name: _____ **Date:** _____

Directions: Find the difference between the three-digit numbers by subtracting the ones, tens, and hundreds.

Assessment - B

1.

Th	H	T	O
	7	2	4
-	3	1	2

2.

Th	H	T	O
	8	5	7
-	5	3	2

3.

Th	H	T	O
	4	3	5
-	1	2	7

4.

Th	H	T	O
	9	4	2
-	3	7	8

5. 999 - 457 = _____

Score

Name:_____ **Date:**_____

Directions: Mentally add 10 to each number in the left column below. Mentally add 100 to the numbers in the right column below. Write your answers on the lines next to the original numbers.

Assessment A

ADD 10	ADD 100

1.
185 _____

6.
551 _____

2.
123 _____

7.
291 _____

3.
337 _____

8.
280 _____

4.
402 _____

9.
462 _____

5.
576 _____

10.
789 _____

Score _____

Name: _____ **Date:** _____

Directions: Mentally subtract 10 from each number in the left column below. Mentally subtract 100 from the numbers in the right column below. Write your answers on the lines next to the original numbers.

Assessment B

SUBTRACT 10	SUBTRACT 100
1. 245 _____	6. 734 _____
2. 832 _____	7. 379 _____
3. 498 _____	8. 937 _____
4. 783 _____	9. 527 _____
5. 487 _____	10. 882 _____

Name:_____   **Date:** _____

Directions: Solve the equations below. Explain, using words or pictures, the strategy you used to solve each problem.

Assessment

How does 7 + 2 help you solve 2 + 7?

Solve: 4 + 2 + 6 = _____

Solve: 43 + 24 = _____

Solve: 78 - 42 = _____

Solve: 335 + 125 = _____

Name: _____ **Date:** _____

Directions: Choose an object in your classroom to measure. Select the best measuring tool for your object. Use the words in the box to complete the recording sheet. Have a partner check your measuring.

Assessment

yardstick   meter stick   ruler   tape measure

inches (in)   centimeters (cm)   feet (ft)

yards (yds)   meters (m)

I measured a _____.

I used a _____.

It was _____ _____ high / long / wide.
      (number)   (unit)

My friend _____ checked my measuring.

good measuring ☐   try again ☐

I measured a _____.

I used a _____.

It was _____ _____ high / long / wide.
      (number)   (unit)

My friend _____ checked my measuring.

good measuring ☐   try again ☐

Score _____

Name: _____ **Date:** _____

Directions: Choose an object in your classroom to measure. Measure it once using inches and again using centimeters. What do you notice about the measurements?

Assessment

I measured a _____.

It is _____ inches long.

It is _____ centimeters long.

I notice that _____

_____.

I measured a _____.

It is _____ inches long.

It is _____ centimeters long.

I notice that _____

_____.

I measured a _____.

It is _____ inches long.

It is _____ centimeters long.

I notice that _____

_____.

Score _____

Name: _____   **Date:** _____

Directions: Choose objects in your classroom to measure. Estimate the length of the objects. Use a different unit of measure for each object you choose.

Assessment

I estimate the _____ is

_____ inches long.   Actual: _____in.

I estimate the _____ is

_____ centimeters long.   Actual: _____cm.

I estimate the _____ is

_____ feet long.   Actual: _____ft.

I estimate the _____ is

_____ yards long.   Actual: _____yd.

I estimate the _____ is

_____ meters long.   Actual: _____m.

Name:_____ **Date:**_____

Directions: Choose two objects of different lengths to measure. Compare the two lengths. Find the difference and record the measurements below. Be sure to include the unit of measure you used.

Assessment

The _____ is _____ _____ long.
　　　　　object　　　　　　　　　number　　unit

The _____ is _____ _____ long.
　　　　　object　　　　　　　　　number　　unit

_____ - _____ = _____

*The _____ is _____ _____ longer.

The _____ is _____ _____ long.
　　　　　object　　　　　　　　　number　　unit

The _____ is _____ _____ long.
　　　　　object　　　　　　　　　number　　unit

_____ - _____ = _____

*The _____ is _____ _____ longer.

The _____ is _____ _____ long.
　　　　　object　　　　　　　　　number　　unit

The _____ is _____ _____ long.
　　　　　object　　　　　　　　　number　　unit

_____ - _____ = _____

*The _____ is _____ _____ longer.

Name:_____ **Date:** _____

Directions: Add or subtract to solve the number stories. You may use drawings and equations to show your work.

Assessment

Carl and Bobby made a long paperclip chain. Carl's part was 13 feet long. Bobby's part was 15 feet long. How long was the entire chain?

_____ft

The train carrying coal is 47 meters long. It is behind another train that is 50 meters long. How long are the two trains together?

_____m

Paula's daisy measures 12 inches long. Patty's daisy grew to be 15 inches long. How much longer is Patty's daisy?

_____in

Brett built a Lego tower that was 67 centimeters tall. It collapsed, and now it is only 32 cm. How many centimeters shorter is the tower now?

_____cm

The first grade class made a human wall that measured 25 yards. The second grade joined them and now the whole wall is 65 yards. How many yards did the second grade add to the wall?

_____yd

Name: _____   **Date:** _____

Directions: Solve the addition and subtraction equations below. Then, draw the symbol for each sum and difference onto the number lines in the appropriate place. Some answers may fall between hash marks. The first one has already been started.

Assessment

⬤ 45 + 15 = _____   ▲ 30 + 25 = <u>55</u>

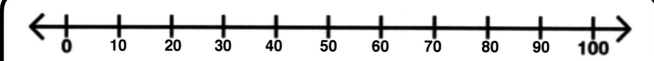

⬤ 33 + 57 = _____   ▲ 38 + 32 = _____

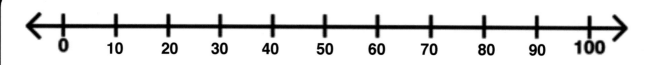

⬤ 85 - 35 = _____   ▲ 70 - 55 = _____

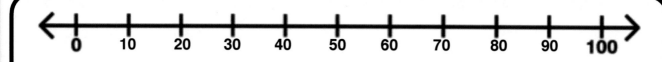

⬤ 88 - 48 = _____   ▲ 71 - 51 = _____

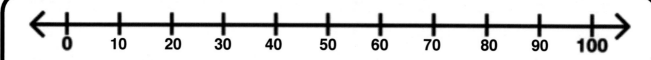

⬤ *42 + 37 = _____   ▲ *76 - 25 = _____

Score [ ]

Name:_____   Date:_____

Directions: Write the times, draw the hour and minute hands, and choose a.m. or p.m. for each clock.

Assessment

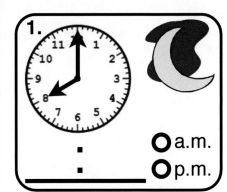
1. ___:___ ○ a.m. ○ p.m.

2. 8:05 ○ a.m. ○ p.m.

3. ___:___ ○ a.m. ○ p.m.

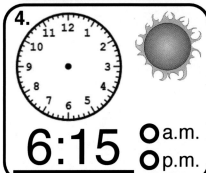
4. 6:15 ○ a.m. ○ p.m.

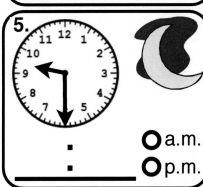
5. ___:___ ○ a.m. ○ p.m.

6. 10:35 ○ a.m. ○ p.m.

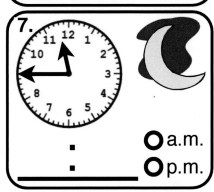
7. ___:___ ○ a.m. ○ p.m.

8. 7:45 ○ a.m. ○ p.m.

9. ___:___ ○ a.m. ○ p.m.

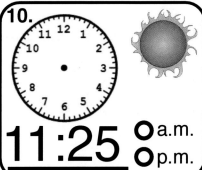
10. 11:25 ○ a.m. ○ p.m.

11. ___:___ ○ a.m. ○ p.m.

12. 9:55 ○ a.m. ○ p.m.

Name:_____ **Date:** _____

Directions: Solve the money number stories below. Use the space to work out the problem. You can draw coins or write an equation. Use the ¢ and $ symbols.

Assessment

When mom vacuumed the couch she found 6 pennies, 5 nickels, and 3 dimes. How much money did mom find?

Sue and Belle collected money for the rescue shelter. At the end of the day they had $7.00 in bills, $2.25 in quarters, and 90¢ in dimes. How much money did the girls collect?

The chocolate bar I want to buy for my dad costs $3.00. I have $5.00. How much change will I get back?

When I left the house, I had $4.35 in my pocket. I lost a quarter and a dime. How much money do I have left?

Mark has 5 dimes and 3 nickels. Steve has 2 quarters and 9 pennies. Who has more money? How much more?

Score

Name: _____ **Date:** _____

Directions: Organize the measurements listed below into a line plot. Use an X to mark the data. Some data points may fall between the hash marks.

Assessment

OBJECT	LENGTH
rope	18 inches
snake	12 inches
scarf	20 inches
stick	6 inches
ribbon	11 inches
shoelace	14 inches
belt	19 inches
backscratcher	13 inches
straw	6 inches

2   4   6   8   10   12   14   16   18   20

Name: _____

Date: _____

Directions: Organize the data below into a pictograph. Then, use the information from the graph to solve the problems.

Assessment A

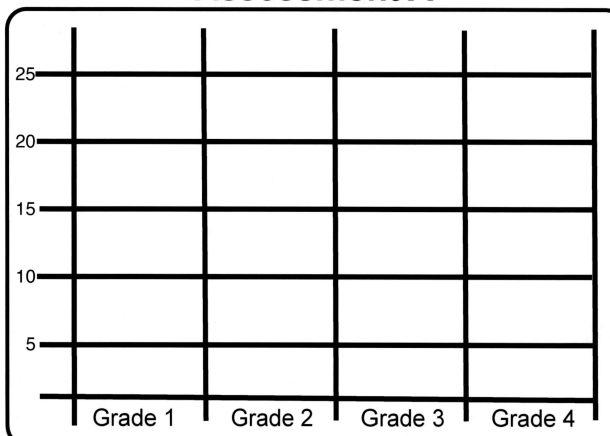

DATA
Grade 1 collected 20 books.
Grade 2 collected 25 books.
Grade 3 collected 15 books.
Grade 4 collected 10 books.

KEY

█████ = 5 books

The school had a book drive to support the local shelter. Grades 1, 2, 3, and 4 collected books. Organize the book data into the pictograph above.

1. Who collected the most books? _____

2. What was the total amount of books collected? _____

3. Which grade collected the least books? _____

Score

Name:_____ **Date:** _____

Directions: Organize the data below into a bar graph. Then, use the information from the graph to solve the problems.

Assessment B

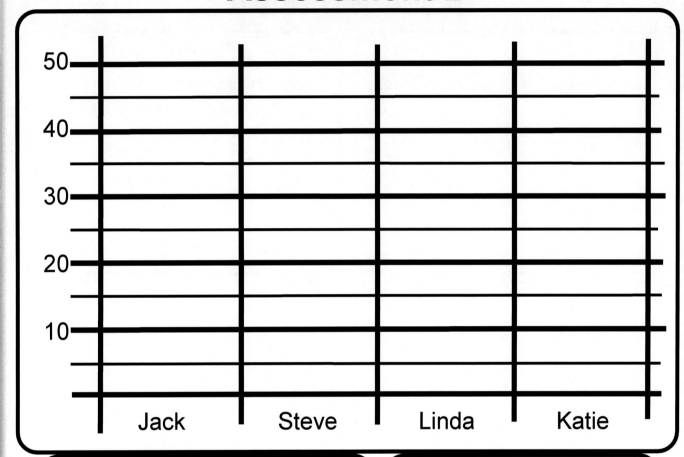

DATA
Jack had 45 candy bars.
Linda had 25 candy bars.
Katie had 32 candy bars.
Steve had 49 candy bars.

KEY

= 5 candy bars

After trick-or-treating, the kids counted their candy. Organize the candy bar data into the bar graph above.

1. Who had the most candy? _____

2. What was the total amount of candy collected? _____

3. How much more candy did Steve get than Linda? _____

Score

Name: _____ **Date:** _____

Directions: Draw shapes below that match the attributes given.

Assessment A

1.
Draw a shape that has 4 equal sides.

2.
Draw a 3D shape that has no straight edges or faces or vertices.

3.
Draw 2 different three-sided shapes.

4.
Draw a 3D shape with only squares for faces.

5.
Draw a shape that rolls.

6.
Draw a shape with 6 sides.

Score [ ]

Name: _____ **Date:** _____

Directions: Choose the correct name for each shape below.

Assessment B

1.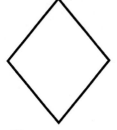
   - ○ square
   - ○ rhombus
   - ○ rectangle

2.
   - ○ square
   - ○ rectangle
   - ○ cube

3.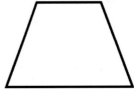
   - ○ trapezoid
   - ○ rhombus
   - ○ rectangle

4.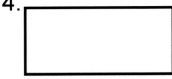
   - ○ circle
   - ○ cube
   - ○ rectangle

5.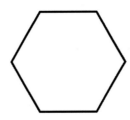
   - ○ pentagon
   - ○ hexagon
   - ○ square

6.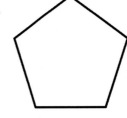
   - ○ octagon
   - ○ rhombus
   - ○ pentagon

7.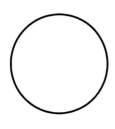
   - ○ square
   - ○ circle
   - ○ cylinder

8.
   - ○ cone
   - ○ triangle
   - ○ cube

9.
   - ○ cone
   - ○ triangle
   - ○ cube

10.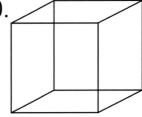
   - ○ square
   - ○ cube
   - ○ trapezoid

Score

Name: _____ **Date:** _____

Directions: Divide these fractions into the indicated fractions, and then answer the questions below the rectangles.

Assessment A

---

1. *Divide this rectangle into 2 equal pieces.*

I cut this rectangle into _____ rows and _____ columns.

This rectangle has _____ equal parts. Each piece is a _____ .

---

2. *Divide this rectangle into 3 equal pieces.*

I cut this rectangle into _____ rows and _____ columns.

This rectangle has _____ equal parts. Each piece is a _____ .

---

3. *Divide this rectangle into 4 equal pieces.*

I cut this rectangle into _____ rows and _____ columns.

This rectangle has _____ equal parts. Each piece is a _____ .

Score [   ]

Name: _____ **Date:** _____

Directions: Divide these fractions into the indicated fractions, and then answer the questions below the rectangles.

Assessment B

1. *Divide this rectangle into 5 equal pieces.*

I cut this rectangle into _____ rows and _____ columns.

This rectangle has _____ equal parts. Each piece is a _____ .

2. *Divide this rectangle into 6 equal pieces.*

I cut this rectangle into _____ rows and _____ columns.

This rectangle has _____ equal parts. Each piece is a _____ .

3. *Divide this rectangle into 8 equal pieces.*

I cut this rectangle into _____ rows and _____ columns.

This rectangle has _____ equal parts. Each piece is a _____ .

Score

Name:_____ Date:_____

Directions: Divide these fractions into as many equal pieces as you want, and then answer the questions below the rectangles.

Assessment C

1. *Divide this rectangle into equal pieces. You choose how many.*

I cut this rectangle into _____ rows and _____ columns.

This rectangle has _____ equal parts. Each piece is a _____ .

2. *Divide this rectangle into equal pieces. You choose how many.*

I cut this rectangle into _____ rows and _____ columns.

This rectangle has _____ equal parts. Each piece is a _____ .

3. *Divide this rectangle into equal pieces. You choose how many.*

I cut this rectangle into _____ rows and _____ columns.

This rectangle has _____ equal parts. Each piece is a _____ .

© http://CoreCommonStandards.com

Score _____

Name: _____ **Date:** _____

Directions: Partition each square according to the directions. Tell how each square is partitioned using words like two halves, three thirds, four fourths.

Assessment A

1.

Partition this square into two equal parts.

The square is cut into _____.

2.

Partition this square into three equal parts.

The square is cut into _____.

3.

Partition this square into four equal parts.

The square is cut into _____.

4.

Partition this square into four equal parts. Make it look different from square 3.

The square is cut into _____.

5. What do you know notice about the 2 squares with 4 equal parts?

_____

Name:_____ **Date:**_____

Directions: Partition each shape according to the directions. Tell how each shape is partitioned using words like two halves, three thirds, four fourths.

Assessment B

1.

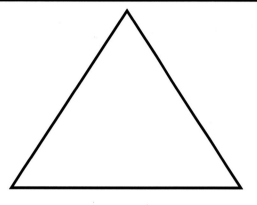

*Partition this triangle into two equal parts.
and color one part purple.*

The triangle is cut into _____.

2.

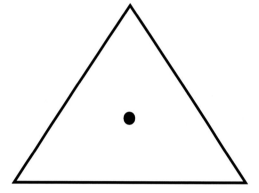

*Partition this triangle into three equal parts
and color two parts red.*

The triangle is cut into _____.

3.

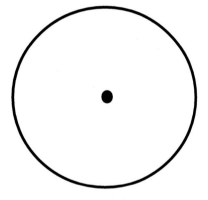

*Partition this circle into two equal parts
and color one part green.*

The circle is cut into _____.

4.

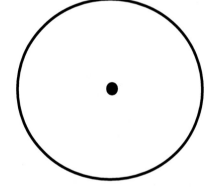

*Partition this circle into four equal parts
and color three parts brown.*

The circle is cut into _____.

5.

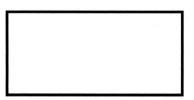

Partition each of these rectangles into a different fraction. Color parts of each.

Common Core State Standards

Progress Reports

Grade 2

- ## Math Standards
- ## English Standards

Worksheets and Activities that assess every standard!

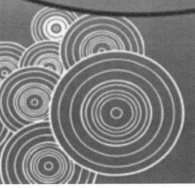

NAME: _____

Use this form to keep track of progress and grades.

Standard	Grade
RL.2.1	/ 5
RL.2.2	/ 4
RL.2.3	/ 9
RL.2.4	/ 14
RL.2.5	/ 6
RL.2.6	/ 6
RL.2.7	/ 6
RL.2.9 1 & 2	/ 8
RL.2.10	/ 6

Standard	Grade
RI.2.1	/ 5
RI.2.2	/ 4
RI.2.3	/ 6
RI.2.4 A	/ 6
RI.2.4 B	/ 9
RI.2.5	/ 9
RI.2.6	/ 8
RI.2.7	/ 9
RI.2.8	/ 5
RI.2.9	/ 10
RI.2.10	/ 6

Standard	Grade
RF.2.3 A	/ 20
RF.2.3 B	/ 20
RF.2.3 C	/ 20
RF.2.4	/ 5

Standard	Grade
W.2.1	/ 6
W.2.2 1 & 2	/ 10
W.2.3 1 & 2	/ 10
W.2.5	/ 10
W.2.6	/ 14
W.2.7	/ 10
W.2.8	/ 4

Standard	Grade
SL.2.1	/ 6
SL.2.2	/ 6
SL.2.3	/ 5
SL.2.4	/ 10
SL.2.5	/ 6
SL.2.6	/ 8

Standard	Grade
L.2.1 A	/ 10
L.2.1 B	/ 10
L.2.1 C	/ 10
L.2.1 D	/ 10
L.2.2 A	/ 10
L.2.2 B	/ 12
L.2.2 C	/ 5
L.2.3	/ 10
L.2.4 A	/ 20
L.2.4 B	/ 15
L.2.5	/ 30
L.2.6	/ 28

NOTES:

NAME: _____

Use this form to keep track of progress and grades.

Standard	Grade
2.OA.1	/ 5
2.OA.2	/ 14
2.OA.3 A	/ 24
2.OA.3 B	/ 15
2.OA.4	/ 18

Standard	Grade
2.NBT.1	/ 27
2.NBT.2	/ 8
2.NBT.3	/ 15
2.NBT.4	/ 10
2.NBT.5	/ 14
2.NBT.6	/ 8
2.NBT.7 A	/ 5
2.NBT.7 B	/ 5
2.NBT.8 A	/ 10
2.NBT.8 B	/ 10
2.NBT.9	/ 10

Standard	Grade
2.MD.1	/ 10
2.MD.2	/ 12
2.MD.3	/ 15
2.MD.4	/ 12
2.MD.5	/ 5
2.MD.6	/ 15
2.MD.7	/ 24
2.MD.8	/ 5
2.MD.9	/ 9
2.MD.10 A	/ 10
2.MD.10 B	/ 10

Standard	Grade
2.G.1 A	/ 6
2.G.1 B	/ 10
2.G.2 A	/ 9
2.G.2 B	/ 9
2.G.2 C	/ 9
2.G.3 A	/ 9
2.G.3 B	/ 11

NOTES:

2

Common Core State Standards

Blank Progress Reports

Grade 2

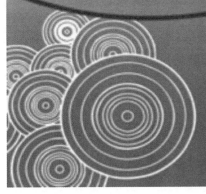

- ## Math Standards
- ## English Standards

Worksheets and Activities that assess every standard!

NAME: _____

Use this form to keep track of progress and grades.

Standard	Grade
RL.2.1	
RL.2.2	
RL.2.3	
RL.2.4	
RL.2.5	
RL.2.6	
RL.2.7	
RL.2.9 1 & 2	
RL.2.10	

Standard	Grade
RI.2.1	
RI.2.2	
RI.2.3	
RI.2.4 A	
RI.2.4 B	
RI.2.5	
RI.2.6	
RI.2.7	
RI.2.8	
RI.2.9	
RI.2.10	

Standard	Grade
RF.2.3 A	
RF.2.3 B	
RF.2.3 C	
RF.2.4	

Standard	Grade
W.2.1	
W.2.2 1 & 2	
W.2.3 1 & 2	
W.2.5	
W.2.6	
W.2.7	
W.2.8	

Standard	Grade
SL.2.1	
SL.2.2	
SL.2.3	
SL.2.4	
SL.2.5	
SL.2.6	

Standard	Grade
L.2.1 A	
L.2.1 B	
L.2.1 C	
L.2.1 D	
L.2.2 A	
L.2.2 B	
L.2.2 C	
L.2.3	
L.2.4 A	
L.2.4 B	
L.2.5	
L.2.6	

NOTES:

NAME: _____

Use this form to keep track of progress and grades.

Standard	Grade
2.OA.1	
2.OA.2	
2.OA.3 A	
2.OA.3 B	
2.OA.4	

Standard	Grade
2.NBT.1	
2.NBT.2	
2.NBT.3	
2.NBT.4	
2.NBT.5	
2.NBT.6	
2.NBT.7 A	
2.NBT.7 B	
2.NBT.8 A	
2.NBT.8 B	
2.NBT.9	

Standard	Grade
2.MD.1	
2.MD.2	
2.MD.3	
2.MD.4	
2.MD.5	
2.MD.6	
2.MD.7	
2.MD.8	
2.MD.9	
2.MD.10 A	
2.MD.10 B	

Standard	Grade
2.G.1 A	
2.G.1 B	
2.G.2 A	
2.G.2 B	
2.G.2 C	
2.G.3 A	
2.G.3 B	

NOTES:

Common Core State Standards

English Answer Keys

Grade 2

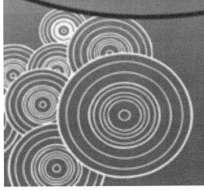

- **Math Standards**
- **English Standards**

Worksheets and Activities that assess every standard!

Reading: Literature

RL.2.1 Assessment

Answers may vary. Sample answers:
1. Morning, during breakfast.
2. Ethan and mom.
3. Ethan eats food that is too sugary, and mom thinks he may get cavities.
4. Eggs, toast, jam, bacon, fruit, milk.
5. Questions may vary.

RL.2.2 Assessment

Answers may vary. Sample answer:
1. The lion saw the mouse as food.
2. He probably feels grateful and respects the mouse.
3. The lion learned that even a small mouse can help a big lion.
4. Don't judge someone by their size. Little friends can be great friends.

RL.2.3 Assessment

Answers will vary, but they should show clear understanding of the stories read, and how events impact characters.

RL.2.4 Assessment

1. line 1 = 7   line 5 = 8
   line 2 = 7   line 6 = 8
   line 3 = 8   line 7 = 7
   line 4 = 8   line 8 = 7

2. cone & alone   creamy & steamy
   drips & hips   round & ground

3. Responses will vary. Look for rhyme and patterning in student writing.

RL.2.5 Assessment

Answers will vary, but they should show clear understanding of the beginning, middle , and end of stories as well as how events relate to each other.

RL.2.6 Assessment

Answers will vary, but should show understanding of different points of view, as well as why different characters have different opinions.

RL.2.7 Assessment

Responses will vary. Students should show an illustration that helps explain the setting, characters, or events in a story. It should have a sensible explanation of how illustrations help them understand a story.

RL.2.9 Assessment - Pages 1 & 2

Answers will vary, but should accurately compare two stories in the following areas: Characters, Settings, Problems, and Solutions.

RL.2.10 Assessment

Students may use this record sheet to record their reading in appropriate grade-level books and poems in various genres and styles.

Reading: Informational Text

RI.2.1 Assessment

Answers may vary. Sample answers:
1. Most giraffes live in Africa.
2. Male giraffes are taller and can grow to 19 feet.
3. They can get water by eating wet leaves.
4. Giraffes are tall, with long necks, long legs, and spotted bodies. They have small horns on top of their heads.
5. Questions may vary.

RI.2.2 Assessment

Answers may vary. Sample answer:
Main Topic: The piñata is a celebration tradition in Mexico.
Paragraph 1: What a piñata is and when it is used.
Paragraph 2: How to use a piñata.
Paragraph 3: The piñata is used by American kids, too.

RI.2.3 Assessment

Responses may vary. Students use this form to record events from an informational story and compare and contrast the events.

RI.2.4 Assessment A

Answers will vary. Student answers should have some sensible meanings, as well as good pieces of evidence to support those meanings.

RI.2.4 Assessment B

Answers will vary depending on stories or texts chosen. Student answers should have some sensible meanings, as well as good pieces of evidence to support those meanings.

RI.2.5 Assessment

Responses may vary. Examples should show the variety of nonfiction text features, and their corresponding page numbers.

RI.2.6 Assessment

Responses may vary.
Responses should describe the author's purpose of the text, and cite examples.

RI.2.7 Assessment

Column 3 answers will vary. Sample answers for columns 1 and 2:
diagram: The image shows the parts of the plant cell. It helps the reader understand how a plant cell is constructed and its various parts.
photograph: The image shows a leaf, its coloring, and its veins. It helps the reader recognize and understand the structure of a leaf.
drawing: The image shows a stem and its leaves. It helps the reader understand how leaves may be grouped on a stem.

RI.2.8 Assessment

Sample answers:
Bowling is fun, full of action (spinning towards white pins, crack of thunder). Colorful shoes, interesting scoring, practice math, great for non-runners, fun with family and friends.

RI.2.9 Assessment

Responses may vary. Students use this form to compare and contrast points from two different texts.

RI.2.10 Assessment

Students can use this checklist to help make sure they read a variety of informational texts.

Reading: Foundational Skills

RF.2.3 Assessment A

street	(long) short	spin	long (short)
kite	(long) short	flute	(long) short
flame	(long) short	scope	(long) short
stun	long (short)	brand	long (short)
stop	long (short)	tent	long (short)

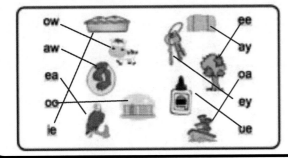

RF.2.3 Assessment B

Color in stars for each correctly read word in both the top and bottom sections.

RF.2.3 Assessment C

Color in stars for each correctly read word in both the top and bottom sections.

RF.2.4 Assessment

Use the form and the directions on the following page to check for reading accuracy and comprehension. Keep a running record of each student's reading progress.

Writing

W.2.1 Assessment

Answers will vary. Students should use this form to explain an opinion about something they have read. Their opinions should be well formed and supported with details.

W.2.2 Assessment - Pages 1 & 2

Answers will vary. Students should use the planning sheet to get facts and details for their writing. On page 2 they can write a draft.

W.2.3 Assessment - Pages 1 & 2

Answers will vary. Students should use the planning sheet to get events and details for their writing. On page 2 they can write a draft.

W.2.5 Assessment

Students should use this form as a checklist for editing and revising their writing.

W.2.6 Assessment

Use this form as a checklist of student computer skills, especially for writing using technology.

W.2.7 Assessment

Students should use this form to take notes on a research project. This sheet can be used as a planning page.

W.2.8 Assessment

Students should use this form to take notes as they search for an answer to a question. The question should be answered at the bottom, using evidence collected.

Speaking & Listening

SL.2.1 Assessment
Responses may vary. Students can use this form when they participate in a group.

SL.2.2 Assessment
Responses may vary. Students can use this form when they listen to an oral presentation.

SL.2.3 Assessment
Responses may vary. Students can use this form when they listen to an speaker.

SL.2.4 Assessment
Students should use this form to plan telling a story or explaining about an experience.

SL.2.5 Assessment
This form can be used to self-critique a presentation with visuals.

SL.2.6 Assessment
This form can be used to check when students are speaking in complete sentences.

© http://CoreCommonStandards.com

Language - Part 1

L.2.1 Assessment A

TOP SECTION:
1. class
2. flock
3. staff
4. stack
5. bouquet

BOTTOM SECTION:
1. myself
2. yourselves
3. herself
4. itself
5. himself

L.2.1 Assessment B

1. men
2. person
3. mice
4. children
5. goose
6. feet
7. tooth
8. oxen
9. woman
10. fish

L.2.1 Assessment C

TOP SECTION:
1. began
2. broke
3. built
4. drew
5. held

BOTTOM SECTION:
1. sadly
2. quickly
3. kind
4. carefully
5. final

L.2.1 Assessment D

Answers will vary. Sample answers:
1. Sally runs fast when she is in a race.
2. The stray cat outside makes noise at night.
3. We are watching a scary movie together on the couch.
4. As I opened my birthday gift, I was thrilled!
5. My mom drinks her hot coffee in a big, goofy mug.

L.2.2 Assessment A

Dear Carlos,

    I am writing to tell you that last week I got a new bicycle. It isn't really new. It used to be Benny's bike, but he bought a new **S**chwinn at **J**oe's **B**ike **S**hop in **E**ast **H**arlem. Benny knew I had asked for a bike for **C**hristmas, but I didn't get one. Wasn't he nice to do that? Now I can give my old bike to Sean before he moves to **N**ew **J**ersey. Sean's bike was stolen last month along with his **D**ell computer. He's upset, and I know this will make him happy! Talk to you soon!

               Your Friend,
               Pedro

L.2.2 Assessment B

Sample Answers:

ICK	UDGE	ART
sick	judge	start
stick	budge	cart
pick	sludge	part
flick	pudge	mart
tick	drudge	smart
quick	fudge	fart

EAT	OAT	IGHT
feat	coat	flight
meat	float	right
wheat	boat	might
heat	goat	tight
treat	moat	light
peat	oatmeal	fight

Language - Part 2

L.2.2 Assessment C

Students should fill in this sheet as they use reference materials. A separate log might be kept to keep track of what they actually used them for.

L.2.3 Assessment

1. informal
2. formal
3. formal
4. informal
5. formal

Sample answers for the bottom:

How wonderful! You received an A on your paper!
It was nice seeing you.
Hope to see you again.

L.2.4 Assessment A

Answers will vary. Sample answers:
TOP SECTION:

Left side:	Right side:
to feel good	to feel bad
to warm up	to warm before
to put on paper	to write again
to be fond of	to be opposed to
to have manners	to have poor manners

BOTTOM SECTION:

Left side:	Right side:
to combine	more of something
to make feel better	To be feeling well at ease
a tall rock	someone who climbs mts
happiness	to be do happily
to leave a mark	feeling about something

L.2.4 Assessment B

Answers will vary. Sample answers:

WORD:	MEANING:
firefly	An insect that lights up
peanut	nut used in peanut butter
handsome	very good looking
bookshelf	a place to store books
birdhouse	a house for a bird

BOTTOM SECTION:

hastily: do quickly
consumed: ate or used
obedient: to obey, follow rules
altered: changed
discarded: threw away

L.2.5 Assessment

TOP SECTION:

peek   glance   look   stare

whisper   say   shout   scream

tiny   small   big   huge

tap   poke   smack   punch

dim   shiny   bright   brilliant

BOTTOM SECTION:
Answers will vary for this section, but should be sensible.

L.2.6 Assessment
Answers will vary, but should be sensible.

Common Core State Standards

Math Answer Keys

Grade 2

- Math Standards
- English Standards

Worksheets and Activities
that assess every standard!

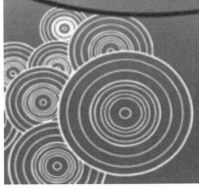

Operations and Algebraic Thinking

2.OA.1 Assessment

1. 15 + 11 = 26 rings
2. 31 - 26 = 5 markers
3. 56 - 24 = 32 bread eaten
4. 24 + 36 - 6 = 54 cookies
5. 89 - 67 = 22 degrees

2.OA.2 Assessment

Answers from left to right.
TOP SECTION:

12	14	14	14
10	14	13	9

BOTTOM SECTION:

15	13	12
8	4	11

2.OA.3 Assessment A

Answers from left to right.
TOP SECTION:
13 blue, 10 red, 60 red, 54 red, 11 blue
27 blue, 15 blue, 18 red, 78 red, 29 blue
41 blue, 24 red, 73 blue, 8 red, 1 blue
83 blue, 92 red, 72 red, 9 blue, 77 blue

BOTTOM SECTION:
Answers will vary.

2.OA.3 Assessment B

Answers may vary depending on how students changed the odd to an even. If they do something other than add 1, the equations below will be different.
Suggested Answers:

ODD/EVEN:	EQUATIONS:
15 odd	8 + 8 = 16
12 even	6 + 6 = 12
9 odd	5 + 5 = 10
14 even	7 + 7 = 14
19 odd	10 + 10 = 20

2.OA.4 Assessment

Responses will vary. Make sure students used 2 different colors to color in sections of each array. The amount of boxes of each color used should be reflected in the addends.

Totals should be as follows:

15	20	25
12	15	10

Numbers and Operations in Base Ten

2.NBT.1 Assessment

Pay special attention to the order of the place values in the answers.

457	**102**	**735**
4 h	2 o	3 t
7 o	0 t	5 o
5 t	1 h	7 h
229	**310**	**864**
9 o	0 o	4 o
2 t	3 h	6 t
2 h	1 t	8 h
983	**658**	**517**
8 t	8 o	5 h
3 o	5 t	7 o
9 h	6 h	1 t

2.NBT.2 Assessment

TOP SECTION:

Make sure students can properly count by 1's for the three ranges:

245-307, 420-463, and 951-1000

BOTTOM SECTION: (blanks only)

80, 85, 90, 100, 105, 110, 115, 120, 125
50, 60, 65, 70, 75, 80, 85, 95, 100, 105
-10, 0, 10, 40, 50, 60, 70, 80, 90, 100
0, 10, 20, 30, 40, 50, 80, 90, 100, 110
100, 200, 300, 500, 700, 800, 900, 1000, 1100

2.NBT.3 Assessment

NUMERALS, WRITTEN, EXPANDED:

75, seventy-five, 70 + 5
136, one hundred thirty-six, 100 + 30 + 6
402, four hundred two, 400 + 2
893, eight hundred ninety-three, 800 + 90 +3
724, seven hundred twenty-four, 700 + 20 +4

2.NBT.4 Assessment

1. >	6. =
2. <	7. >
3. >	8. <
4. =	9. <
5. <	10. <

2.NBT.5 Assessment

Answers from left to right.
TOP SECTION:

56	90	59	89
66	61	25	13

BOTTOM SECTION:

45	64	88
33	41	81

2.NBT.6 Assessment

1. 46   2. 77   3. 78   4. 86
5. 146   6. 108   7. 76   8. 113

2.NBT.7 Assessment A

1. 779	2. 859
3. 444	4. 1,242
5. 898	

2.NBT.7 Assessment B

1. 412	2. 325
3. 308	4. 564
5. 842	

2.NBT.8 Assessment A

1. 195	6. 651
2. 133	7. 391
3. 347	8. 380
4. 412	9. 562
5. 586	10. 889

2.NBT.8 Assessment B

1. 235	6. 634
2. 822	7. 279
3. 488	8. 837
4. 773	9. 427
5. 477	10. 782

2.NBT.9 Assessment

Answers may vary. Sample answers:
1. They are the same but reversed. Both = 9
2. 4 + 6 = 10 and 2 more is 12.
3. (40 + 20) + (3 + 4) = 67
4. 78 - 40 = 38, minus 2 more = 36.
5. 335 + 100 = 435 + 25 = 460

Measurement and Data

2.MD.1 Assessment
Answers will vary according to objects chosen. Check for accuracy and understanding of measurement.

2.MD.2 Assessment
Answers will vary according to objects chosen. Check for accuracy and understanding of measurement.

2.MD.3 Assessment
Answers will vary according to objects chosen. Check for accuracy and understanding of measurement.

2.MD.4 Assessment
Answers will vary according to objects chosen. Check for accuracy and understanding of measurement.

2.MD.5 Assessment
1. 13 + 15 = 28 ft
2. 47 + 50 = 97 m
3. 15 - 12 = 3 in
4. 67 - 32 = 35 cm
5. 65 - 25 = 40 yds

2.MD.6 Assessment
1. green 60, blue 55
2. green 90, blue 70
3. green 50, blue 15
4. green 40, blue 20
5. green 79, blue 51

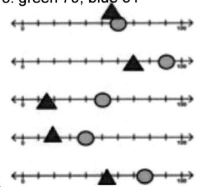

2.MD.7 Assessment
Check hour and minute hand positions.

1. 8:00 pm   2. ↗ am   3. 7:10 am

4. ↳ am   5. 9:30 pm   6. ↓ am

7. 11:45 pm   8. ↘ am   9. 7:20 pm

10. ↘ am   11. 8:50 pm   12. ↙ am

2.MD.8 Assessment
1. 6 + 25 + 30 = 61 cents
2. 7 + 2.25 + .9 = $10.15
3. 5 - 3 = $2.00
4. 4.35 - (.25 + .10) = $4.00
5. MARK = 50 + 15 = 65 cents
   STEVE = 50 + 9 = 59 cents
   So, Mark has more money.

2.MD.9 Assessment
Check for proper locations of the X's.
X's should be located at :
6, 6, 11, 12, 13, 14, 18, 19, 20

```
        X
        X      X X X X       X X X
_____
  2   4   6   8  10  12  14  16  18  20
```

2.MD.10 Assessment A
Check to make sure the graph is completed correctly.
1. grade 2
2. 70 books
3. grade 4

2.MD.10 Assessment B
Check to make sure the graph is completed correctly.
1. Steve
2. 151 bars
3. 24 bars

Geometry

2.G.1 Assessment A

Possible shapes to draw:
1. square or rhombus
2. sphere
3. choose two of: right, scalene, isosceles, acute, obtuse, and equilateral triangles
4. cube
5. sphere or cylinder
6. hexagon

2.G.1 Assessment B

1. rhombus	2. square	3. trapezoid
4. rectangle	5. hexagon	6. pentagon
7. circle	8. triangle	10. cube
	9. cone	

2.G.2 Assessment A

1. I cut this rectangle into <u>2</u> rows and <u>1</u> column. **OR**
 I cut this rectangle into <u>1</u> row and <u>2</u> columns.
 This rectangle has <u>2</u> equal parts. Each piece is a <u>half</u>.
2. I cut this rectangle into <u>3</u> rows and <u>1</u> column. **OR**
 I cut this rectangle into <u>1</u> row and <u>3</u> columns.
 This rectangle has <u>3</u> equal parts. Each piece is a <u>third</u>.
3. I cut this rectangle into <u>2</u> rows and <u>2</u> columns. **OR**
 I cut this rectangle into <u>4</u> rows and <u>1</u> column. **OR**
 I cut this rectangle into <u>1</u> row and <u>4</u> columns.
 This rectangle has <u>4</u> equal parts. Each piece is a <u>fourth</u>.

2.G.2 Assessment B

1. I cut this rectangle into <u>5</u> rows and <u>1</u> column. **OR**
 I cut this rectangle into <u>1</u> row and <u>5</u> columns.
 This rectangle has <u>5</u> equal parts. Each piece is a <u>fifth</u>.
2. Combinations of rows and columns should be: 1 & 6, 6 & 1, 2 & 3, or 3 & 2
 This rectangle has <u>6</u> equal parts. Each piece is a <u>sixth</u>.
3. Combinations of rows and columns should be: 1 & 8, 8 & 1, 2 & 4, or 4 & 2
 This rectangle has <u>8</u> equal parts. Each piece is a <u>eighth</u>.

2.G.2 Assessment C

Answers will vary. For these problems, make sure that students have correctly cut the rectangles into fractions of equal pieces. They must then count the rows and columns correctly, and then identify what fraction they have made.

2.G.3 Assessment A

Make sure all of these fractions have been cut into equal-sized pieces.
1. halves
2. thirds
3. fourths
4. fourths
5. They are both fourths, even if they are cut differently.

2.G.3 Assessment B

Make sure all of these fractions have been cut into equal-sized pieces.
1. halves (1/2 is colored purple)
2. thirds (2/3 is colored red)
3. halves (1/2 is colored green)
4. fourths (3/4 is colored brown)
5. All three should be different fractions, and they should be colored.

Common Core State Standards
Educating classrooms one standard at a time.

Terms of Use

Fore more Common Core Standards Posters, Activities, Worksheets, and Workbooks, visit http://CoreCommonStandards.com.

Worksheets created by: Have Fun Teaching
Activities created by: Have Fun Teaching
Posters created by: Have Fun Teaching

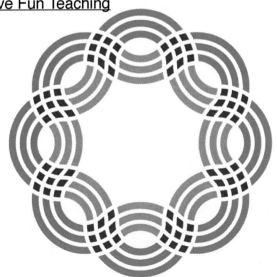

Made in the USA
Las Vegas, NV
19 September 2023